Animal Life Cycles

Contents

What is a life cycle?

Penguin

A life cycle shows us how an animal grows – from the time it is a tiny egg until it is fully grown. All animals change as they grow. Some animals change just a little. Others change a lot!

Salmon

Butterfly

Frog

This book tells you about the life cycle of nine animals. Which one do you want to find out about?

Eagle

Turtle

Seahorse

Kangaroo

Elephant

Salmon

start

The female salmon lays her eggs in a river.

After two to four years, the fry becomes a fully grown salmon. It swims back to the river where it was born.

Two years after hatching, each fry swims down the river to the sea. This is its new home.

The eggs hatch into tiny fish called fry. Each fry feeds on an egg sac.

The fry lives and feeds in the river. It grows bigger and stronger.

Salmon timeline

8

7

6

5 — Salmon 4 years

4

3

2 — Fry 3 years

1

Egg 4 months

0

Years

Frog

start

In the spring, the female frog lays her eggs in a pond. The eggs are called frogspawn.

After three years, the froglet becomes an adult frog.

The tadpole changes into a tiny frog called a froglet. It leaves the pond and lives on land.

The frogspawn hatches into tiny black tadpoles.

Each tadpole begins to change. It gets bigger and begins to grow legs.

Frog timeline

Frog
2 years

Froglet
3 years

Tadpole
9 weeks

Egg
2 weeks

6

5

4

3

2

1

0

Years

Butterfly

start

The female butterfly lays her eggs on a plant.

An adult butterfly crawls out of the chrysalis.

The caterpillar turns into a chrysalis. Inside, its body begins to change.

The eggs hatch into tiny caterpillars.

Each caterpillar feeds on plant leaves. It grows very fast.

The fully-grown erpillar stops eating.

Butterfly timeline

13
12
11
10
9
8
7
6
5
4
3
2
1
0

Months

Butterfly
10 months

Chrysalis
3 weeks

Caterpillar
5 weeks

Egg
3 weeks

Penguin

start

The female penguin lays an egg in winter. The male penguin keeps it warm in a pouch above his feet.

After one year, the chick becomes an adult penguin.

The chick begins to grow its waterproof feathers. Soon it will be able to swim and catch fish.

The egg hatches into a fluffy chick. It moves into its mother's pouch.

The mother feeds her chick on fish. It soon grows too big for the pouch.

20

15

10

5

0

Years

Penguin
19 years

Chick
9 months

Egg
9 weeks

Turtle

The female turtle lays her eggs in a hole in the sand.

After ten years, the turtle is fully grown.

The turtle lives in the sea. It feeds on tiny creatures and grows bigger and stronger.

Each egg hatches into a tiny turtle. It digs its way out of the sand.

Each turtle crawls down to the sea.

Turtle timeline

65
60
55
50
45
40 — Adult turtle
       50 years
35
30
25
20
15
10 — Young turtle
       10 years
5
0 — Egg
     2 months

Years

13

Kangaroo

start

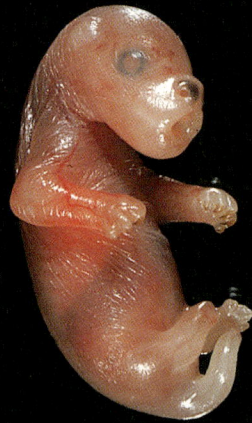

The baby kangaroo develops from an egg inside its mother's body. When the baby is born, it is very tiny.

After one year, the joey becomes a fully grown kangaroo.

The joey begins to leave the pouch and feed on grass.

Kangaroo timeline

The baby is called a joey. It crawls into its mother's pouch and feeds on her milk.

After four months, the joey is fully developed but it still rides in the pouch.

8
7
6
5 — Kangaroo 7 years
4
3
2
1 — Joey 1 year
0 — Developing baby 1 month

Years

Eagle

start

The female eagle lays her eggs in a big nest called an eyrie.

After five years, the young eagle becomes a fully grown eagle.

A young eagle has all its feathers. It can now fly.

The eggs hatch into chicks called eaglets. They are small and very fluffy.

The parents feed their young. The eaglets grow bigger and stronger.

Eagle timeline

35
30
25
20 — Adult eagle 25 years
15
10
5 — Young eagle 5 years
— Eaglet 6 months
0 — Egg 6 weeks

Years

17

Seahorse

start

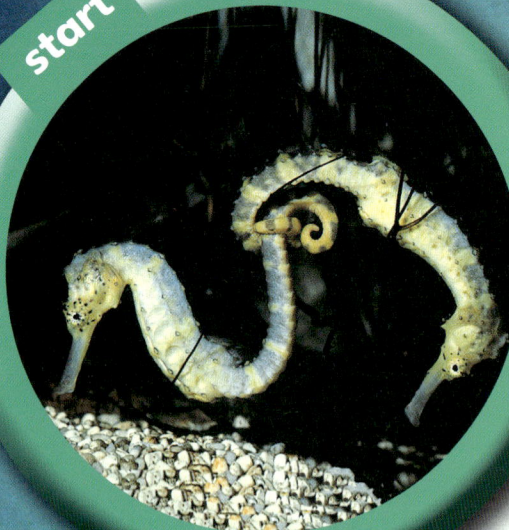

The female seahorse lays her eggs in the male's pouch. The eggs develop inside the pouch.

The seahorse grows bigger and stronger. After one year, it is fully grown.

After twenty-one days, the eggs hatch into tiny seahorses.

The baby seahorses look after themselves. They feed on tiny creatures in the sea.

Seahorse timeline

Years	
7	
6	
5	Adult seahorse 5 years
4	
3	
2	
1	Young seahorse 1 year
0	Egg 21 days

Elephant

start

The baby African elephant develops from an egg inside its mother's body. It is born after twenty-two months.

The calf becomes a fully grown elephant at the age of thirteen.

20

The baby elephant is called a calf. It feeds on its mother's milk.

The elephant calf lives in the herd. Its mother teaches it everything it needs to know.

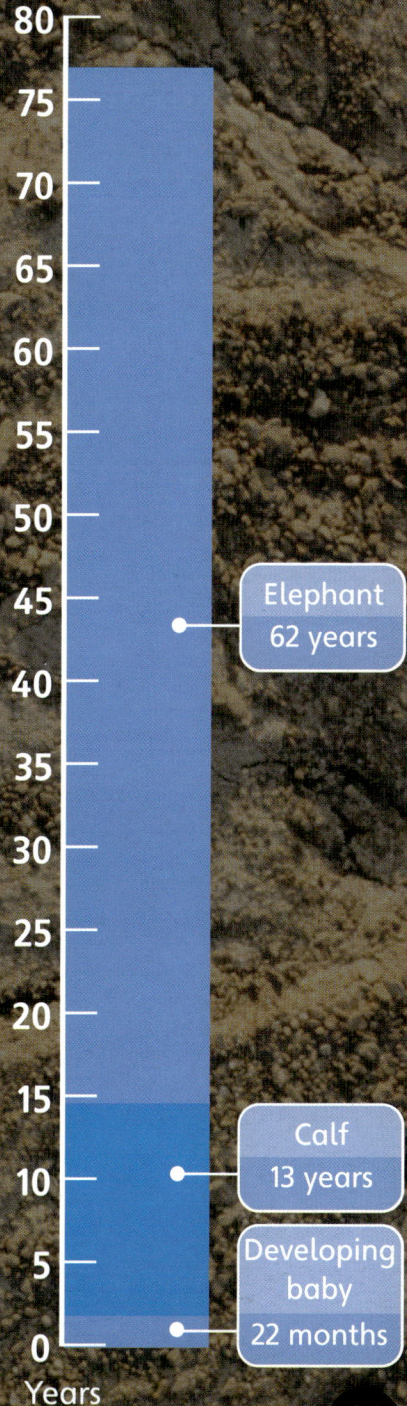

Elephant timeline

Elephant
62 years

Calf
13 years

Developing baby
22 months

Years

Animals and their young

ANIMAL YOUNG	Butterfly	Frog	Salmon	Penguin
Hatches out of an egg	✔	✔	✔	✔
Develops inside its mother				
Needs its parents				✔
Lives on land	✔	✔		✔
Lives in water		✔	✔	

Turtle	Kangaroo	Eagle	Seahorse	Elephant
✔		✔	✔	
	✔			✔
	✔	✔		✔
	✔	✔		✔
✔			✔	

Index